TWO STALWART SCOTTISH CRICKETERS JOHN KERR and JIMMY AITCHISON

by

Duncan McLeish

First published in Great Britain by
Association of Cricket Statisticians and Historians
Cardiff CF11 9XR

British Library Cataloguing-in-Publication Data.
A catalogue record for this book is available from the British Library.

ISBN: 978 1 905138 65 4
Typeset by Limlow Books

Introduction

Anyone researching the history and statistics of Scottish cricket will be struck by the frequency with which a certain two names crop up. These are John Kerr and the Rev James (Jimmy) Aitchison. Both made their mark in the Scottish game, particularly as batsmen, Kerr in the first third of the 20th century, Aitchison in the second. Though of course there have been other notable cricketers who were born in Scotland, these were perhaps the two most famous who spent all their cricketing careers in their native land. Of course, in the sphere of global cricket they would hardly be regarded as famous or important, but I felt that they were significant enough in a more limited sphere for something to be written and published about them; hence this work.

The Men

John Kerr

John Kerr c1910

The Kerr family were prominent in Greenock for much of the nineteenth and twentieth centuries. Their main interests were in shipping, engineering, sugar refining and ironfounding, in a town noted for such activities. John Kerr himself was mainly involved with J.&R. Houston and Kerr Limited, Ironfounders, of Cartsburn Foundry, Greenock. However, it was not only in such industries that the Kerrs were prominent, for in 1946 N.L. Stevenson wrote in *Play!* that 'The Kerrs of Heathfield, Westfield and Heywood have figured with distinction in Glenpark annals for over 70 years.' Glenpark has been the home of Greenock Cricket Club since 1864, and it was at Heywood, in Margaret Street, a very short distance from Glenpark, that John Kerr was born on 8 April, 1885. It was to remain his home for virtually all of his long life. With its fine façade it still overlooks the esplanade and the Firth of Clyde.

John's father, Daniel, is given as 'Shipowner' on John's birth certificate, though he is elsewhere listed as 'merchant' and 'commission agent'; and his mother was Margaret, *nee* McNeidy. Dan himself was a noted and enthusiastic cricketer, keen and able to impart his own undoubted skills to his family; and he and his sons, James, Robert and John, were stalwarts of Greenock, and indeed Scottish, cricket over many years. Consequently John, as he grew up, moved easily into the Greenock cricket scene, initially appearing for the first eleven of Greenock CC at the age of fifteen. He was then still attending the local Collegiate School, where he had come under the tutelage of A.L. Graham, a fine allrounder with the Greenock Club, who added to the skills and enthusiasm already imparted by John's father. This selection was no hollow honour, for Greenock were then, and always have been, one of the top

***Heywood*, John Kerr's imposing lifelong home, still overlooks the waterfront at Greenock**
(Author)

club sides in Scottish cricket, and John Kerr was undoubtedly to become their greatest player, apart of course from such noted 'Test' professionals as Gordon Greenidge.

As he grew into adulthood, John became more involved in the running and directing of the Kerr business empire. Of that empire there is little or no trace in Greenock today. Though Cartsburn Foundry, with its associated Glenburn Engineering Works, was closed in the 1920s, Kerr still thereafter concerned himself in his other business interests; and it would appear that he still had plenty of time to spend on cricket. His obituary in the *Greenock Telegraph* remarked that 'He was a man of some means, and so he was able to lead the kind of life that is denied to most. But he never obtruded this. He did not allow it to raise a barrier between himself and others.' One can read all kinds of things between these lines. However, from oral tradition it would appear that, while John Kerr may have done his best not to flaunt his abundant means and free time, there were those who would say something like, 'No wonder he is good at cricket, he has plenty of time to practise.' There would also seem to have been the feeling that, since Kerr was unmarried, he had even more time to spend on the cricket field. In addition he had some success in his youth on the rugby field and the badminton court, badminton being a very popular sport in the Inverclyde area. In any case, at the time of Kerr's youth cricket was *the* summer game for many Scots, though golf was beginning to have an effect. Greenock CC was, and still is, a very well supported club, and with his father, brothers and cousins involved in the game and the Club it is little wonder that John too soon became a devotee.

However, John Kerr devoted his spare time to much more than cricket, for the Church of Scotland and its various associated activities took up even more of his time. He was a lifelong member of St George's Church, Greenock. He became an elder there and for 27 years represented it on Greenock Presbytery, where he served on a number of committees. From there he was commissioned on a number of occasions to serve as a member of the Church's supreme court, the annual General Assembly. There he took part in debates and served on various of its committees. He was a pioneer of education courses for elders. That too was at a time when such a position within the Church conferred considerable status on a man, and even for this John would have been a prominent figure in the town.

In addition to his administrative work for the Church, John Kerr was also deeply involved with the 7th Greenock (St. George's Church) Boys' Brigade Company. He was associated with that company for 53 years, firstly as lieutenant, and then for 40 years as captain. There he gained the nickname of 'The Skipper' to add to his cricketing ones of 'The Wee Man' and 'The Greenock Guv'nor'. He was praised for his modesty, tolerance, good humour and regard for the young, to whom he always tried to set a good example, whether in the Boys' Brigade hall or on the cricket field.

In that connection John Kerr was noted as being a very abstemious man, though he seems to have loosened the reins a little in later life. At any rate he does not seem to have grudged his colleagues their refreshment. However, he was less equable with regards to smoking, for against that he conducted a fierce campaign in the teeth of scepticism, when the dangers of the habit were virtually unknown.

Cricketing days over, John Kerr turned his active sporting participation to bowls, at the Ardgowan Club, again close to his home at Heywood. Not that he completely neglected cricket, for he became an honorary vice-president of the Scottish Cricket Union (SCU), Scottish cricket's governing body, having served on some of its committees. Though he had set various records in Scottish international cricket, he was always delighted when someone broke them. For Jimmy Aitchison recalled that, when he broke one of Kerr's records, John always congratulated him, either in person at the ground or by telegram. Kerr managed to attend most of Scotland's representative matches, and just before his death it was announced at the Annual General Meeting of the SCU that he had donated £200 towards the expenses of Scotland's annual match against Ireland at Greenock in the previous summer.

Death came to John Kerr at the age of 87 in a Greenock hospital on 27 December, 1972. On the next day the *Greenock Telegraph* carried three separate obituaries to John Kerr: a general one, one from the Boys' Brigade, and one from T.C. Riddell, the historian of Greenock cricket. In addition, the newspaper itself devoted a leading article to him. At his funeral on 2 January, 1973, when the Rev W.B. Johnston spoke of John's 'simple and uncomplicated faith', the mourners at St George's Church included civic dignitaries, as well as those from the Church, Boys' Brigade and the Scottish cricket world. Kerr was then buried in Greenock Cemetery on Bow Hill. As the *Telegraph* editorial had remarked, John Kerr was physically a small man, but in mind and spirit a great one; and, even apart from his cricket, 'he achieved - and will keep - a place in the hearts of his fellow townsmen.'

Jimmy Aitchison

Jimmy Aitchison

James Aitchison's father, also called James, was a noted cricketer in Kilmarnock before World War 1. Although that conflict resulted in him losing an arm and a leg, he continued his off-the-field activities with Kilmarnock Cricket Club. So, like John Kerr, Jimmy Aitchison was born into a family where there was already interest and ability in cricket. James Sr., a tobacconist, and doubtless disapproved of by John Kerr, had married Elizabeth Mackie, and their son James was born on 26 May, 1920, in Kilmarnock, an Ayrshire town noted for the production of whisky, carpets and railway locomotives. James was the young Aitchison's only Christian name, even though *Wisden* at various times designated him as J.A., J.K. and J.S.; the *Almanack* seemed to find one initial not enough for certain 'Gentlemen of Scotland' or 'Gentlemen of Ireland' cricketers.

Jimmy's first home was at 30 Witch Road, near the centre of Kilmarnock. His early cricketing development was fostered not only by his father, but also by his mother, who bowled to him in the space behind their home. That early home, with all the houses and shops on that side of Witch Road, has, however, been demolished in recent years, to be replaced by sheltered housing, on roughly the same configuration as the old buildings. The present number 30 is in a block called Thomson Court; how appropriate it would have been to have called it Aitchison Court. The open area behind it, where the young Aitchison practised his batting, is still there, but has been securely fenced off.

Jimmy's first appearance in a match of any significance was at the age of 13, when he played for Kilmarnock Juniors in a local 'derby' against their Ayr counterparts. Alas, in the presence of his

A modern block occupies the site of 30 Witch Road, though there is still some open ground behind it where the young Aitchison practised.

(Author)

father, he was bowled third ball for a duck. Nearly 20 years later he wrote, 'Ah well, better to learn the lesson young. A man can never have a better start than adversity. I have seen too many youngsters destroyed by an overdose of prosperity in their early careers.'

The old pavilion at Kirkstyle, Kilmarnock, that witnessed Jimmy Aitchison's first duck, and John Kerr's last century. It was superseded by a new pavilion in 1959, and demolished in 1974. However, that pavilion, and the ground, are now under a supermarket.

By that time Jimmy was attending Kilmarnock Academy, where he had a distinguished academic career. Even in the 1930s cricket would have been the main summer team sport there, and matches would have been played against the leading schools in the West of Scotland. Indeed in recent years Kilmarnock CC have made use of the Academy's playing facilities.

At some point Jimmy decided that his future lay in the full time ministry in the Church of Scotland, and in 1938 he went up to Glasgow University. There he distinguished himself again in the academic sphere, gaining the degrees of Master of Arts and Bachelor of Divinity. He also made his mark in the allround sporting area and, as Fraser Simm remarks, 'was an impeccable sportsman, maintaining modesty as well as fitness'. However, since his debut for the Kilmarnock first eleven in 1938, cricket had been Jimmy's first sporting love.

Even so, as with many other young men of his time, both his cricket and academic careers were interrupted by the onset of World War 2. During that conflict he served with the Church of Scotland's 'Huts and Canteens' activity, and drove one of the Church's lorries at the D-Day landings in 1944. Consequently it was 1947 before he completed his probationership for the ministry, and was ordained and inducted to the charge of Renton Union Church in the industrial Vale of Leven in Dunbartonshire.

There, as one of his obituarists noted, he 'tirelessly ministered to the people'. However, he found time on summer Saturdays to continue his cricketing career, firstly with Kilmarnock Cricket Club, where he gained his first Scottish 'caps'. While there seems to be no record of parishioners complaining about him spending his Saturday afternoons playing cricket, when he should have been writing sermons, conducting marriages, or whatever, human nature being what it is, it is likely that there were grumbles.

As a clergyman who played cricket, there are inevitably stories of him being 'blessed' and receiving 'divine providence' with regard to lbw decisions; though he himself had another explanation as far as lbw decisions were concerned, as noted below. One enduring story comes from Ronnie Chisholm, Aitchison's Scotland batting colleague, who recalled that in a match against Worcestershire, possibly that of 1951, Roly Jenkins bemoaned Jimmy's continual luck with regard to both edges and decisions. The bowler remarked that, with his kind of luck, Jimmy would become Archbishop of Canterbury, an office of course that is firmly closed to clergy of the Kirk. On the cricket field too Jimmy received his nicknames of 'The Rev' and 'Aitchie'. Even so, his ministerial status may have been a barrier that kept some players at a distance from him, if oral tradition is to be believed.

After six years at Renton Jimmy was elected to the charge of St Stephen's Church, Comely Bank, a residential area to the west of the centre of Edinburgh. This is quite close to Raeburn Place, the home of Grange Cricket Club, the 'MCC of Scotland'. Though Aitchison did play occasionally for that prestigious club, he played rather more regularly for their Edinburgh rivals, Carlton CC. He seems to have felt that travel to turn out for Kilmarnock was out of the question, for he played but little there until 1959. Even so, he found time to write *Kilmarnock Cricket Club: One Hundred Not Out*, where, despite his efforts to play down his own part, his own exploits inevitably featured largely.

His ministry in Edinburgh seems to have been a distinguished one, and it is perhaps surprising that in 1963 he applied for and was elected to the charge of Broomhill, another residential area, this time in the west side of Glasgow. Perhaps it was coincidence, but Broomhill is quite close to Scotland's second most noted ground, Hamilton Crescent, the home of West of Scotland CC. By that time, however, Jimmy was back playing regularly for Kilmarnock. In later years he did play for West of Scotland second eleven, but refused to turn out against Kilmarnock.

After his retirement from international cricket, Aitchison, unlike John Kerr, seems to have taken no part in the administration of the game; perhaps his ministerial responsibilities dictated otherwise. However, he was present at the Glasgow Titwood ground in 1991 to congratulate Iain Philip on his 234 against MCC, the record score by a Scottish international. Philip also surpassed Aitchison's record aggregate of runs in Scottish international matches.

Jimmy remained at Broomhill Church until his retirement from the full-time ministry in 1986. He went to live in Newton Mearns, a town in Renfrewshire, just to the south-west of Glasgow. Even then he still took an active part in Church activities at the Broomhill Church. He also devoted much time to his children and, in later years, to his grandchildren. For, unlike John Kerr, he was a married man. He and his wife Catherine, whom he married in 1947, had two daughters, Mary and Elizabeth.

Jimmy Aitchison died, after a long illness, at the Beatson Oncological Institute, Glasgow, on 13 February, 1994, being survived by his wife and daughters. His funeral service in the Broomhill Church was followed by cremation in Glasgow. At the next meeting of Glasgow Presbytery the Rev Derek Haley paid tribute to him as a minister who would be 'remembered for years to come'. He noted that 'Jim Aitchison was very much a "people's man" and saw himself first and foremost as a parish minister'. His obituary in *The Scotsman* noted that he was among 'the mere handful of Scottish cricketers whose recognition extends beyond these shores'. As late as 1992 he had been invited to be guest of honour at the annual cricket festival at St George's, Bermuda, 'where he had clearly made a lasting impression as a visiting player'. That also cemented the cricketing links between Scotland and Bermuda, the latter having sent three long-serving professionals to the former: Alma Hunt, Nigel Hazel and Clarence Parfitt, Hunt and Parfitt both representing Scotland in internationals.

The Cricketers

John Kerr

As previously mentioned, John Kerr had first played for the Greenock first eleven in 1900 at the age of 15. In the following year, when he would have left school and the supervision of A.L. Graham, he came under the tutelage of W.H. Jenner, Greenock's professional, who seems to have influenced him greatly, and for whom he had the greatest regard; as indeed he had for professional cricketers in general. So, in consequence of this reinforcement of the efforts of Dan Kerr and A.L.Graham, there began a career that was to produce 21,558 runs, with 49 centuries, plus about 300 wickets, in all cricket; and was to end in 1940.

Kerr first came to the notice of the Scottish selectors at the age of 18 in 1903, when he achieved little against Gilbert Jessop's XI. His maiden first-class match was in 1908, when he was selected in the last season before the present Scottish Cricket Union was established, and when the international sides were selected by a committee on which the Grange CC had the biggest say. Hence the 1903 and 1908 matches are not regarded as official 'caps', though present historians award notional 'caps' for such matches. In any case the Greenock youngster again had a poor match, this time against Nottinghamshire, and dropped out of the international scene until 1913.

However, he was still piling up the runs on the club scene. While his club cricket was normally with Greenock, Kerr also represented Carlton CC, particularly on their tours, scoring centuries for them on their Highland expeditions to Inverness. He also toured the Isle of Man with Carlton, and in 1905 he scored two centuries for Stafford, and in 1911 two for Hampstead, to which English places duty seems to have taken him.

He returned, with rather more success, to the international scene before World War 1 brought a virtual stop to his cricket career, though he is recorded as having played some cricket at Greenock during that conflict, when little cricket of any importance was played. His firm, being ironfounders, were probably engaged in war work; and, with Kerr being what nowadays would be regarded as its managing director, his presence in Greenock is hardly surprising. On the return of peace, there was a renewed taste of international cricket when Kerr played three two-day matches against the strong Australian Imperial Forces side. His 40 not out, for a 'Scottish Union' side, on a crumbling wicket against the likes of Gregory and Collins was reckoned by some, including indeed Kerr himself, as one of his best innings. Another candidate for that honour was his innings two years later against the mighty touring Australians, when he scored 147 to save the game for Scotland. Others still rank his best innings as that of 137 against Ireland in 1928, when he completed his 1,000 runs against that country, which had often felt the weight of his bat. His international career came to an end in 1933.

However, John continued on his merry way for Greenock, where his contributions as captain and batsman ensured that the club was usually at or near the top of the Western Union championship table. In 1938 he scored his last century for Greenock at Kirkstyle, Kilmarnock. Jimmy Aitchison remarks that it was 'a turning point in my own cricket career, for there I had the privilege of fielding at point during John Kerr's last Union 100 and observing the man who had written his name across Scottish cricket. The lessons... [instilled in me]...about running between the wickets were finally accepted through that innings which shone with strokes and judgement.' Aitchison continues: 'It is a great man who has performed such deeds on a cricket field as he did; but it is a greater who can be consistently encouraging to one who had performed similar deeds in perhaps more favourable circumstances. Among my souvenirs are treasured telegrams from John Kerr.'

Indeed John Kerr had previously attracted the notice of an even greater batsman than Aitchison, namely Jack Hobbs. who ranked him as one of the world's greatest batsmen. He found the time to come to Greenock in 1935 with H.B. Rowan's XI to play the home side which included Kerr. The latter, aged 50, scored 61, while the 52 year old Hobbs had 62.

Kerr and Hobbs pictured together at Greenock in 1935; it is obvious why Kerr was nicknamed 'the wee man'.

Five years later, in 1940, Kerr ended his career in a wartime match at Whitehaugh, Paisley, scoring 58. He continued to take an interest in the affairs of Greenock CC, becoming its honorary president from 1956 until his death; and indeed, as noted above, he concerned himself with the SCU too until just before his death.

Surviving descriptions of Kerr's batting compare it, appropriately perhaps, to 'the precision of a first-class engineering job'. Initially, he would have been regarded as an orthodox right-handed batsman for his time, concentrating on the off side, with splendid square or late cuts, the latter being his favourite stroke. His batting then seems to have been carefree and little concerned about where the fielders were stationed. Opposing bowlers of course became wise to such tactics, packed the off-side field and bowled accordingly. Then Kerr, after assiduous practice in the nets, changed his method; and with brilliant footwork moved across to hook or pull into the unguarded on-side field. Even if bowlers tried to plug the gaps, he would then play over the fielders' heads, or into the spaces that they had just vacated; but always with an eye to safety. At times, according to N.J.Gibson of Greenock CC, he seemed 'more mechanical than human', and his 'hypnotic influence on a young bowler was a chastening and demoralising experience'. At any rate, to his faith in himself and his sound technique, which all batsmen should have, Kerr had added abundant courage and a spirit of adventure.

John Kerr posing to show his technique

Some may have felt that his concentration and thirst for runs showed him to lack warm feeling and the 'understanding of the true cricketer'. However, as he himself later remarked, in 1959, 'When playing cricket, nothing mattered but the challenge, but now I can catch up on the neglected side of the game which I find more fruitful and enduring.'

Nor did Kerr excel only in batting, for he was a fine fielder, particularly at slip. He himself described his slow right-arm bowling as 'donkey drops'. However, these were sometimes successful enough, for in the 1921 match against the Australians he took three wickets in eight balls after his first 18 had gone for 32. On slow or soft Scottish wickets even the high flighted ball may bounce but little, and so evade the flailing bat of the unwary batsman.

Jimmy Aitchison

Aitchison's debut in the Kilmarnock juniors was an inauspicious one. However, he worked his way up through the elevens and made his first-team debut against Greenock, and John Kerr, at Kilmarnock in 1938. In that year too Harold Riley came from Leicestershire to be professional at Kilmarnock, and to reinforce the foundations laid by Jimmy's father and mother. A club professional then had to have qualities as a coach, as well as being a consistent contributor with bat and/or ball on the field of play; competency at groundsmanship was an added recommendation. Riley's batting, off-spin bowling and fielding were very impressive, but Aitchison also praised him for his patient demeanour, noting that: 'As a coach he was excellent, knowing the game well, keen to impart it, but never intruding opinions except when they were keenly sought. He taught me leg side play, how to drop the ball on the leg stump and guide it away for runs. "Don't glide, Jimmy," he used to say, and I am sure it is due to his teaching that my very small proportion of lbw's is due.'

Obviously a model professional and model pupil, Jimmy Aitchison seems to have had as high a regard for the club professionals at Kilmarnock as John Kerr had for those at Greenock. Riley's batsmanship seems to have had a great effect on Aitchison, but so indeed did his fielding skills; for Aitchison was a very fine fielder, and in the outfield his accurate returns to the stumps were noted. He bowled but little, even less than John Kerr, occasionally purveying right-arm medium pace. However, in Aitchison's book *Kilmarnock Cricket Club*, Hugh Fulton, in a tribute to its author, claims that Jimmy was 'a useful right or left-arm bowler with some command of pace and spin'. Unfortunately, he does not enlarge on this intriguing statement.

Even at an early stage, 'It was now abundantly clear that something in the nature of a comet rather than a star was blazing forth at Kirkstyle' (Kilmarnock CC's then ground). Moreover, his progress had been noted elsewhere in Scotland. However, before he could move further towards the international arena, World War 2 intervened. The return of peace brought Jimmy Aitchison his first Scottish cap, against India in 1946, when he was the only Scots batsman to resist the visiting spinners. He was to be a fixture, apart from absences due to injury or professional commitments, until 1963, when his total of 69 Scottish caps was a record.

Aitchison was captain of Kilmarnock CC from 1948 to 1950, when the club won or shared the Western Union Cricket Championship. The fact that Jimmy was captain for three successive, and successful, seasons vindicated the stance that he had made against the club's policy of moving the captaincy around annually. Yet, despite his success at Kilmarnock, Aitchison never captained his country. As it happened, there were a number of other strong candidates for the captaincy during Aitchison's years in international cricket: W.A.Edward, Hunter Cosh, Jimmy Brown.

Like John Kerr, Jimmy Aitchison was a highly competitive right-handed batsman, with good footwork and a keen eye, despite his always wearing spectacles. Like Kerr again, he was an orthodox player initially, and would let his left leg strike the ground with considerable force, as he executed his characteristic off or straight drives. Again bowlers became wise to him and, like Kerr, he was persuaded to develop his leg side shots, being particularly strong on hooking the short-pitched ball, though with grace and rhythm. Fulton noted too that Aitchison did indeed execute almost every stroke in the book with efficiency, having an almost unerring choice of stroke, due to picking up the ball's flight early. According to Fulton, Aitchison's most majestic stroke was his cover drive: 'This is a scintillating display of the coordination of eye, mind, wrist and feet. There is first, and distinctly discernible, the gleam of recognition of a ball to be hit; there is the fleet footed skip down the wicket, the simultaneous flash of bat, arms and teeth; the thud as the ball meets bat; and the florid follow-through that gives the speeding ball its penetrative path to the boundary.'

Later, another Kilmarnock player was to note that Aitchison was 'perhaps not the most elegant of batsmen, but certainly one of the most determined and vigilant. Some contended, probably rightly, that his bat was not always in the classical position, but it was invariably there when the ball arrived.' So basically the picture of Jimmy is one of an orthodox batsman, initially strong on the off side, but prepared to take risks to push the score along; much like John Kerr, he also developed a strong leg-side repertoire.

Aitchison's obituarist in *The Scotsman* noted that even in England his ability and highly competitive attitude were recognised, Freddie Trueman having recently recalled an encounter when Yorkshire were on the receiving end of an Aitchison century, in 1952. It was presumably on that occasion too that John Wardle suggested to Aitchison, as he neared his century, that he might donate his wicket to Wardle after that landmark. However, Aitchison went on to 150, when Wood got his wicket.

Kilmarnock Cricket Club, Western District Cricket Union champions in 1959. Six of its members, denoted by asterisks, won international honours for Scotland:
Back Row (l-r): T.A.B. Shedden, *J. Thomson, K. Brice, *R. Ellis, J.M. Clark;
Middle Row: J.H. Sinclair, *T.N. Gallacher, J.W. Craig, O. Graham, M.S. Jamieson, *R.G. Hill, H. Fulton;
Front Row: J. McWilliam, *J. Aitchison, J.R. McCulloch, *A. Johnston, J.G. Fraser, T. Bell

As noted previously, Aitchison played but little for Kilmarnock in the years 1952-1958, due to his ministerial duties in Edinburgh, where his club cricket was played mainly with Carlton CC, with occasional forays with Grange: two clubs with whom John Kerr had also played from time to time. During these years, in 1956, Jimmy played what is possibly his most famous innings: his 100 for Scotland against the Australians in Glasgow. He had already scored a century against the 1947 South Africans, and that feat of scoring a century against two major touring sides surpassed even John Kerr's effort. He was to score seven centuries in all for Scotland, five at first-class level.

Towards the end of his international career in 1963, Aitchison played against the young Mike Denness in the Ayr CC, and with him for Scotland, thus forming a continuity between Kerr and Denness. Thereafter Jimmy continued to play for Kilmarnock, to whom he had returned in 1959. He continued to play regularly until in 1967 he seemed to have ended his career with a typically hard hitting 55 against Kelburne. He did, however, turn out occasionally for West of Scotland second eleven, refusing, as noted, to play against Kilmarnock. Indeed, when the latter side were suffering from a shortage of players in 1973, due to injuries, Jimmy stepped in to play three matches for them. Thus finally ended a career that had produced 31,051 runs in all cricket, with 56 centuries.

R.H.E.Chisholm (left) and J.Aitchison walking out to the wicket to resume Scotland's innings against Middlesex at Raeburn Place on June 28 1962.
The former was caught after making 83,
while Aitchison was 78 not out when the innings was declared.

The Australians

The Australian touring sides of 1921 and 1956 both paid a visit to Scotland. In each of these years a Scot scored a century against them: respectively John Kerr and Jimmy Aitchison, in two innings notable in the history of Scottish cricket.

1921

John Kerr's century against the 1921 Australians was not his first encounter with an Australian side, however. In 1919 he had played in four matches against the strong Australian Imperial Forces side. For the Western District of Scotland in Glasgow he had scored 17 and 8, but for the Scottish Union in Edinburgh he had 45 and 40 not out. This last innings was on a crumbling wicket, and indeed was reckoned on a par with his century two years later. Kerr had another 17 for an XI of Scotland against the AIF, then on August 13 in Greenock he represented his home side's Select XI in a one-day match and scored 103 out of his team's total of 183.

The 1921 Australians were reckoned as a very great side, and before they met Scotland only two centuries had been scored against them: by Hubert Ashton and Philip Mead. Their first match with Scotland was at Glasgow on July 9 and 11 against a West of Scotland side, from which Kerr was surprisingly omitted, apparently to let in George Gunn and Arthur Carr of Nottinghamshire as 'honorary' Scots. However, at Perth on July 12 and 13 Kerr was included in the Scotland side and scored 15 and an unbeaten 60. While Kerr's score was creditable, the Australians rested their front-line bowlers as the match was destined for a draw.

The mini-series was resumed at Raeburn Place, Edinburgh, on July 14 and 15. On the first day the Australians, with six of the eleven who had played in the Third Test a week or so earlier, rattled up 514 all out, with centuries from Collins and Andrews; though Bob Sievwright (3/116) and Kerr (3/37) bowled creditably.

The Australians opened the bowling with Gregory and Armstrong, and perhaps not surprisingly Kerr played himself in 'with marked caution', as *The Scotsman* put it; before lunch he had a run of 14 singles. After lunch, when Mailey and Ryder bowled, Armstrong had placed a silly mid-on to Kerr, who gradually drove him back. Indeed *The Glasgow Herald* remarked that his 'beautiful placing to leg' was a feature of Kerr's innings. He may have given a chance to Hendry in the slips, but the fielder made no contact with the ball. More palpable was a stumping chance off Mailey when Kerr had scored 17, but Oldfield broke the stumps without the ball in his hands. Hendry himself had caused Kerr problems with his fast-medium bowling.

However, Kerr and Gilbert Alexander put on 109 for the fifth wicket, the latter scoring an 'attractively-played 60'. His half-century had come in 70 minutes with eight fours. As *Wisden* remarked, Kerr 'played a rigidly defensive game till he had passed his 100, his big score including 53 singles.' A boundary off Mailey brought up Kerr's century, and thereafter he scored more freely. He looked to be lasting out the day when, however, he fell lbw to Andrews for 147. His innings, with 12 fours, had lasted four hours eight minutes, and had been accumulated at about half the rate that the Australians had scored. Not that that would have worried the crowd of about 8,000; about the same as on the first day, the total receipts being about £1,500. Then as now a match against Australia was very popular, with capacity crowds and healthy financial returns.

The match had been effectively saved for Scotland by their captain's innings; the highest up till then for Scotland, beating the 91 against the Irish in 1909 by Leslie Balfour-Melville, the 'W.G. Grace of Scotland '. The bat which Kerr used in the match still hangs in Greenock CC's pavilion at Glenpark, with a plate commemorating the feat and the contribution of John Kerr and his brothers to Greenock cricket.

Rather oddly, neither *The Scotsman* nor *The Glasgow Herald* was particularly generous with regard to praising Kerr's innings. They rightly lauded Alexander's contribution, but were at pains to point out the missed chances off Kerr. Perhaps a pointer may come in *Play!* by Dr. N.L. Stevenson, who was presumably at the match. He noted that there, and at Perth, there was a lack of purpose about the Australians' cricket. Apparently at one point an Australian fielder made a play of reading a newspaper, though that may have been when the match was undoubtedly heading for a draw. So perhaps the press may have felt that Kerr's success, though creditable, was rather a hollow one.

Be that as it may, the Scot's innings was praised by the Australian captain, Warwick Armstrong, who later wondered why the English Test selectors had not picked Kerr for the Tests. The simple answer of course is that the thought almost certainly never crossed their minds. For all that, Kerr's innings was significant then, as now, in Scottish cricket history, being Scotland's first century against the Australians.

Against the 1926 Australian tourists Kerr scored 31 and 0 for the West of Scotland, and 18 and 11 in the main match at Edinburgh. In 1930, in a rain ruined first-class match at Edinburgh, he scored 20; and then 25 for a Scottish XI at Glasgow. So in 15 innings, two not out, against the various Australian sides, Kerr had totalled 557 at an average of 42.85. Even if all but one of the matches were non first-class, and the Australian sides may have been relaxing a little, it is still a creditable performance, showing that John Kerr could rise to the occasion; and it reflects well against his average in international and indeed club cricket.

1956

Before his century against the Australians in 1956 Jimmy Aitchison had played four two-day matches against previous Australian tourists. In 1948 he had scored 25 not out and 5, then 32 and 9, the last scores being in Don Bradman's triumphant farewell to British cricket at Aberdeen. In 1953, in three innings Aitchison had the poorish scores of 13, 9 and 3. However, his performances against the visiting South Africans had been rather more convincing. For in 1947 he had scored an unbeaten 106, and four years later a fine 55.

The 1956 Australians, who were undoubtedly weaker than the 1921 and 1948 sides, played two matches in Scotland, the first at Hamilton Crescent, Glasgow, on 12, 13 September, some two weeks after they had lost the Fifth Test, and the Ashes, at The Oval. Of that side seven appeared in Glasgow. Unusually, the crowd was a disappointing one for a match against the Australians, but many were doubtless kept away by the threatening weather.

Lindwall opened the bowling with Crawford, but Miller soon replaced the latter. Scotland's first wicket fell at 22, when Aitchison came to the crease. He scored fairly slowly against the pace bowlers, but he and Barr put on exactly 50 before the latter fell. Aitchison was an undefeated 40 when play was suspended for rain and bad light at 3.10, the day's play being finally abandoned at 4.30.

There was much overnight rain, and more threatened, so the second day crowd was again restricted. Play was delayed by 35 minutes because of a 'muddy' outfield and run-ups. One suspects that, had this been a first-class match, it would not have started at all. Possibly because of that, or possibly because he felt that the match was dead anyway, Keith Miller, captaining the Australians in place of Ian Johnson, did not immediately deploy Lindwall and himself. In all he used nine bowlers, including wicket-keeper Gil Langley; Richie Benaud took over the gloves. *The Glasgow Herald* implied that some in the crowd regarded Miller as 'condescending' in employing such tactics.

Be that as it may, Jimmy Aitchison seized his chance, taking only 55 minutes to get the 60 runs that made up his 'carefree' century. During that time 75 runs were added, only six coming from batsmen other than Aitchison. He scored nine fours and two sixes, one of the latter being a massive straight drive over the sightscreen off Langley. When Jimmy was in the 80s, Miller decided to make things that much more difficult for him, and himself returned to bowl with Lindwall. Richie Benaud tells us that Miller's first bouncer caused Aitchison to fall to the ground as he avoided it, but his next two were hooked peremptorily to the square-leg boundary. Both batsman and bowler seemed to enjoy this passage of arms as Jimmy succeeded in reaching his century; but was then bowled by Lindwall with the new ball. His innings had lasted just over three hours.

On leaving the crease Aitchison received the personal congratulations of John Kerr, the only previous scorer of a century for Scotland against an Australian side. The Scots were soon all out for 196. When the Australians batted, they ran up 328 all out, passing Scotland's score in two and a half hours with four wickets down, though there were no centuries. There was no time for further play. So, as the match was over two days, it was officially drawn. Television cameras were at the match; and *The Glasgow Herald* wrongly claimed that this was the first such occasion, for they had shown part of a club match at the Shawholm ground in Glasgow in the previous season.

After his triumph in Glasgow Jimmy Aitchison was brought down to earth over the next two days at Aberdeen. There he could only manage 8 and 2 against the same opposition. In the first innings he was caught by Langley, whose bowling he had thrashed in Glasgow. Langley also bowled at Aberdeen, even taking a wicket.

Thus in ten innings, one not out, against these opponents Aitchison had scored 206 runs at an average of 22.96; not as good as Kerr's performance, but creditable enough against what were still strong sides. Moreover, Benaud, Lindwall and Miller at various times made favourable comment about Aitchison's performance, as Warwick Armstrong had done about John Kerr's. The Australians may have regarded such matches as 'informal', as *The Scotsman* put it, but they could still recognise a quality batsman when they saw one.

The Matches

John Kerr's and Jimmy Aitchison's match details are divided into convenient periods, usually of four or five years. Within each period there is division into first-class and non first-class matches, the former being given a reference number, the latter a letter. Summaries and comments come at the end of each period. Details for each match conform to the following pattern (l-r):

Match number /letter; details of Kerr's/Aitchison's dismissal; his score; Scotland's score; opponent's score; Kerr's/Aitchison's bowling analysis (O-M-R-W), with details of dismissals; Kerr's/Aitchison's catches.

That pattern is repeated for second innings, as appropriate.

John Kerr

1903-1914

First-Class

	Own	Team Totals	Opp	Bowling	Ct
1 Scotland v Nottinghamshire at Raeburn Place, Edinburgh, June 15, 16, 17, 1908 Nottinghamshire won by six wickets					
c A.O.Jones b T.G.Wass	0	215	194		c N.V.C.Turner
c G.T.Branston b T.G.Wass	0	133	155/4		
2 Scotland v Oxford University at The Parks, Oxford, June 9, 10, 11, 1913 Oxford University won by 34 runs					
c P.H.Davies b B.G.V.Melle	44	178	214		c A.C. Williamson c P.H. Davies
b J.N. Fraser	21	152	150		
3 Scotland v Surrey at The Oval, London, June 12, 13, 14, 1913 Surrey won by seven wickets					
c J.W.Hitch b T.Rushby	10	250	142		c H.Strudwick
run out	8	155	264/3		
4 Scotland v Ireland at Raeburn Place, Edinburgh, July 10, 11, 12, 1913 Draw					
not out	64	224	224		
c P.F.Quinlan b R.J.H.Lambert	22	228/8	368/5d	17-2-48-2 P.F.Quinlan b A.C.Bateman	c R.J.H.Lambert c W.Eddie
5 Scotland v Ireland at Rathmines, Dublin, July 16, 17, 18, 1914 Scotland won by 11 runs					
c P.F.Quinlan b G.W.F.B.Kelly	28	224	249		
c J.A.Donnelly b W.W.Meldon	74	207	171		

	M	*I*	*NO*	*R*	*Ave*	*HS*	*100*	*50*	*O*	*M*	*R*	*W*	*Ave*	*BB*	*Ct*
1908-1914	5	10	1	271	30.11	74	0	2	17	2	48	2	24.00	2/48	5

Non First-Class

	Own	Team Totals	Opp	Bowling	Ct
A Scotland v G.L.Jessop's XI at Raeburn Place, Edinburgh, July 13, 14, 1903 Draw					
lbw b C. LTownsend	3	227	263		
did not bat	-	82/3	201		
B Scotland v Northamptonshire at Forthill, Dundee, August 1, 2, 1913 Draw					
b W.Wells	36	172	308	1-0-8-0	
b J.V.Murdin	35	250/8	233/2d		

The 18-year-old Kerr began his international career in 1903 against G.L.Jessop's scratch eleven, but achieved little. Five years later Kerr made an even more inauspicious start to his first-class career with a pair, batting at No.8. He of course was not unique in this, and at least took one catch. That was Scotland's last match under the old dispensation, where the national side was selected by a committee dominated by the Grange Club of Edinburgh, 'the MCC of Scotland'. Thereafter Scottish cricket was under the control of the Scottish Cricket Union, with representatives from member clubs nationwide. Even so, the SCU did not see fit to select the young Greenock batsman for yet another five years, when his performances for his club forced him back into international contention. The expedition to England in 1913 brought mixed returns. Then two matches against Ireland showed Kerr's potential as he attained his best score so far in each of the matches, and had some success with his bowling and fielding. Unfortunately of course World War 1 then put a stop to Kerr's international career for yet another five year period.

1919-1923

First-Class

	Own	*Team Totals*	*Opp*	*Bowling*	*Ct*
6 Scotland v Ireland at Raeburn Place, Edinburgh, July 22, 23, 24, 1920 Scotland won by nine wickets					
c B.J.Ward b R.J.H.Lambert	3	218	142		c B.J.Ward
not out	62	137/1	211		
7 Scotland v Ireland at Rathmines, Dublin, August 4, 5, 6, 1921 (Captain) Draw					
lbw b W.Allen	11	109	186		c A.P.Kelly
not out	22	42/6			
8 Scotland v MCC at Lord's, London, June 7, 8, 9, 1922 (Captain) MCC won by an innings and 183 runs					
lbw b D.Roberts	15	229	576/6d	11-0-58-2 C.H.Titchmarsh J.Hardstaff	(c C.H.T.) c and b c M.Patten
c J.Hardstaff b R.D.Busk	9	164			
9 Scotland v Surrey at The Oval, London, July 14, 15, 16, 1922 (Captain) Draw					
c T.F.Shepherd b H.A.Peach	54	173	303/8d	5-0-22-1 B.W.Bullock	c A Sandham st S.M.Sturgeon
			209/6		c B.W.Bullock
10 Scotland v Ireland at Hamilton Crescent, Glasgow, July 13, 14, 15, 1922 (Captain) Draw					
c D.R.Piggott b W.Pollock	75	297	275	8-0-58-1 W.Pollock	c C.E. McAusland c N.D.Noble
c D.R.Piggott b R.J.H.Lambert	7	165	185/6	4-0-20-0	
11 Scotland v Ireland at Trinity College Park, Dublin, June 21, 22, 23, 1923 (Captain) Draw					
not out	178	372	170		
b J.G.Heaslip	17	51/6	294	1-0-4-0	
12 Scotland v Surrey at Hamilton Crescent, Glasgow, July 7, 9, 10, 1923 (Captain) Draw					
c H.Strudwick b C.Thain	26	187	433		c H.A.Peach c H.S.Harrison
b A.Jeacocke	23	137/9	191/6d		
13 Scotland v Wales at The North Inch, Perth, July 21, 23, 1923 (Captain) Wales won by an innings and 111 runs					
c H.Spencer b J.Mercer	11	61	357	1.4-0-11-1 D.Sullivan	c T.A.L.Whittington c G.W.A.Alexander
c H.Spencer b F.P.Ryan	60	185			
14 Scotland v Middlesex at Raeburn Place, Edinburgh, July 30, 31, August 1, 1923 (Captain) Draw					
c E.H.Hendren b G.T.S.Stevens	7	147	210		
lbw b F.J.Durston	5	132/6	131/5d		

	M	*I*	*NO*	*R*	*Ave*	*HS*	*100*	*50*	*O*	*M*	*R*	*W*	*Ave*	*BB*	*Ct*
1920-1923	9	17	3	585	41.78	178*	1	4	30.4	0	173	5	34.60	2/58	9
1908-1923	14	27	4	856	37.21	178*	1	6	47.4	2	221	7	31.57	2/48	14

Non First-Class

	Own	Team Totals	Opp	Bowling	Ct
C Scotland v Australian Imperial Forces at Raeburn Place, Edinburgh, July 2, 3, 1919 (Captain) Draw					
b J.Gregory	45	266	350		
not out	40	79/8			
D Scotland v Australians at The North Inch, Perth, July 12, 13, 1921 (Captain) Draw					
b E.A.McDonald	15	162	422		c H.L.Collins c E.R.Mayne
not out	60	79/0			
E Scotland v Australians at Raeburn Place, Edinburgh, July 14, 15, 1921 (Captain) Draw					
lbw b T.J.E.Andrews	147	294/8	514	4.2-0-37-3 J.Ryder b H.S.T.L.Hendry st D.B.Bissett W.A.Oldfield c R.E.Batson	

After World War 1 Scotland's first international outing was in a two-day match against the AIF: his first match as Scottish captain, a post he held for 20 matches, 15 of them first-class. Kerr acquitted himself with credit in that match, and also in what was his first match as an opener for Scotland: against Ireland in the next year. In the second innings of the Irish match he had his first century stand, an unbroken 102 with John Grieve. One would have expected many such stands in Kerr's career, but for a century stand to take place the main scorer has to have at least a modicum of support from his partner. That was largely unforthcoming in Kerr's career, apart from the contribution of Gilbert Alexander, the Aberdeenshire captain. 1921 saw two non first-class matches against the touring Australians, detailed above. His second innings at Perth was highly regarded, even when compared with his century at Edinburgh. Kerr had a century stand against the Irish in the next year, with the annual foes also feeling the weight of his bat in 1923. He continued to do some occasional good work with his 'donkey drops', but he did little bowling after 1923; by which year both his career batting and bowling averages had been on the increase.

1924-1928

First-Class

	Own	Team Totals	Opp	Bowling	Ct
15 Scotland v South Africans at Hamilton Crescent, Glasgow, May 31, June 1, 2, 1924 (Captain) South Africans won by an innings and 286 runs					
c C.D.Dixon b D.J.Meintjes	5	36	389/5d	2-0-31-0	
b C.D.Dixon	10	67			
16 Scotland v Ireland at Forthill, Dundee, July 19, 21, 22, 1924 Draw					
c C.E.McAusland b W.Allen	3	178	134		c J.G. Heaslip c C.E.McAusland
			128/7		
17 Scotland v Wales at St Helen's, Swansea, August 23, 25, 26, 1924 Wales won by an innings and 79 runs					
b F.P.Ryan	24	150	307/6d		
b F.P.Ryan	9	78			
18 Scotland v Lancashire at Old Trafford, Manchester, May 13, 14, 1925 (Captain) Lancashire won by an innings and 74 runs					
c R.K.Tyldesley b C.H.Parkin	0	52	321		c J. Sharp
lbw b R.K.Tyldesley	31	195			
19 Scotland v Ireland at Trinity College Park, Dublin, July 11, 13, 14, 1925 Ireland won by 179 runs					
lbw b J.G.Heaslip	29	281	364		
b E.L.Kidd	10	179	275/6d		
20 Scotland v Ireland at Glenpark, Greenock, July 10, 12, 13, 1926 Scotland won by an innings and 147 runs					
b L.Walker	137	464/9d	210 107		c E.A. Barry c D.C. Pickeman

	Own	Team Totals	Opp	Bowling	Ct
21 Scotland v Ireland at Trinity College Park, Dublin, July 9, 11, 12, 1927 Draw					
c L.Bookman b T.H.Dixon	67	129	245		c T.G.B.McVeigh c C.M.Hill
bT.H.Dixon	136	290/8d	173/4		
22 Scotland v Ireland at Raeburn Place, Edinburgh, July 7, 9, 10, 1928 (Captain) Draw					
b T.H.Dixon	52	211	346		c A.P.Kelly
st A.P.Kelly b W.C.Pemberton	137	302/9	221/5d		

	M	*I*	*NO*	*R*	*Ave*	*HS*	*100*	*50*	*O*	*M*	*R*	*W*	*Ave*	*BB*	*Ct*
1924-1928	8	14	0	650	46.42	137	3	2	2	0	31	0	-	-	8
1908-1928	22	41	4	1506	40.70	178*	4	8	49.4	2	252	7	36.00	2/48	22

Non First-Class

	Own	*Team Totals*	*Opp*	*Bowling*	*Ct*
F Scotland v Yorkshire at Hamilton Crescent, Glasgow, May 1, 2, 1924 (Captain) Draw					
did not bat	-	17/1	267		c R.Kilner
G Scotland v South Africans at Raeburn Place, Edinburgh, May 29, 30, 1924 (Captain) Draw					
c P.A.M.Hands b E.P.Nupen	2	177	186		
not out	80	163/4d	59/2		
H Scotland v The Australians at Raeburn Place, Edinburgh, July 21, 22, 1926 Draw					
st W.A.Oldfield b C.V.Grimmett	18	94	563		c W.M.Woodfull
lbw b J.M.Taylor	11	106/4			
I Scotland v New Zealanders at Hamilton Crescent, Glasgow, June 24, 25, 1927 Draw					
run out	18	233	90/2		

After a rain-ruined two-day match against Yorkshire in 1924, 'Kerr did himself full justice' in his second innings against the South Africans in the two-day match; but failed in the following first-class match, which was a disaster for both Kerr and Scotland. He did little better that year in the matches against the other Celtic countries, though Wales were in fact virtually all players from the Glamorgan team, then hardly a dominant power in county cricket.

1925 was also a year of little success for Scotland, but the following three years saw Kerr at his best in the matches against the Irish, with all of his five scores in the 50-150 range. In 1926 he played a characteristic innings, his 'placing on either side of the wicket being particularly skilful', as he put on a double-century opening stand with Parker. Next year he batted 'admirably' for four hours, though Ireland required only two runs to win when time was called. In 1928 another 'great effort' was necessary to save the game for Scotland, as he put on 123 in an opening stand with Stevenson, thereby scoring his one thousandth run against Ireland. All that activity further boosted his career average over the 40 mark.

1929-1933

First-Class

	Own	*Team Totals*	*Opp*	*Bowling*	*Ct*
23 Scotland v Ireland at Trinity College Park, Dublin, July 6, 8, 9, 1929 (Captain) Scotland won by nine wickets					
c A.J.H.Robinson b P.A.Thornton	36	340	145		c J.B.Ganley
not out	7	18/1	212		c T.H.Dixon
24 Scotland v South Africans at The North Inch, Perth, July 20, 22, 23, 1929 (Captain) South Africans won by an innings and 5 runs					
st E.A.van der Merwe b Q.McMillan	42	148	297		c H.G.O.Owen-Smith
c E.A.van der Merwe b N.A.Quinn	17	144			
25 Scotland v Ireland at Mannofield, Aberdeen, July 21, 23, 1930 Scotland won by ten wickets					
c R.J.Barnes b E.Ingram	88	316	145		c M.Sugden
did not bat	-	14/0	184		

26 Scotland v Australians at Raeburn Place, Edinburgh, July 16, 17, 18, 1930 Draw

lbw b C.V.Grimmett	20	129/3		

27 Scotland v Ireland at Trinity College Park, Dublin, July 27, 29, 30, 1931 (Captain) Ireland won by 72 runs

lbw b J.MacDonald	23	101	124	c E.Ingram
lbw b T.H.Dixon	9	118	167	

28 Scotland v New Zealanders at Hamilton Crescent, Glasgow, July 15, 16, 17, 1931 New Zealanders won by 235 runs

b A.M.Matheson	35	112	176	c T.C.Lowry
lbw b W.E.Merritt	20	110	281/7d	

29 Scotland v Ireland at Glenpark, Greenock, June 18, 20, 21, 1932 (Captain) Ireland won by 58 runs

c F.J.A.Reddy b E.Ingram	59	325	242	c P.O'M.Dixon c A.C.Douglas
c T.H.Dixon b J.C.Boucher	23	177	318	

30 Scotland v South Americans at Raeburn Place, Edinburgh, July 7, 8, 9, 1932 Scotland won by eight wickets

lbw b F.F.Keen	10	345	220	
not out	39	84/2	208	

31 Scotland v Indians at Forthill, Dundee, July 23, 25, 26, 1932 Indians won by 200 runs

lbw b M.Nissar	5	81	146	
lbw b M.Nissar	22	110	245	

32 Scotland v Ireland at Ormeau, Belfast, June 17, 19, 20, 1933 Ireland won by 23 runs

c J.MacDonald b H.R.Morgan	13	109	159	
c J.C.Boucher b A.C.Douglas	1	141	114	c A.C.Douglas

	M	*I*	*NO*	*R*	*Ave*	*HS*	*100*	*50*	*O*	*M*	*R*	*W*	*Ave*	*BB*	*Ct*
1929-1933	10	18	2	469	29.31	88	0	2	-	-	-	-	-	-	9
1908-1933	32	59	6	1975	37.26	178*	4	10	49.4	2	252	7	36.00	2/48	31

Non First-Class

	M	*I*	*NO*	*R*	*Ave*	*HS*	*100*	*50*	*O*	*M*	*R*	*W*	*Ave*	*BB*	*Ct*
1903-1927	9	13	3	510	51.00	147	1	2	5.2	0	45	3	15.00	3/37	4

All matches for Scotland

	M	*I*	*NO*	*R*	*Ave*	*HS*	*100*	*50*	*O*	*M*	*R*	*W*	*Ave*	*BB*	*Ct*
1903-1933	41	72	9	2485	39.44	178*	5	12	55	2	297	10	29.70	3/37	35

As John Kerr moved into his mid-forties his powers began to wane. As is evident from the match details, he was frequently trapped leg before wicket; perhaps evidence that his footwork was not as good as it had been. There were no centuries during this last period. Even so he managed an opening stand of 150 in the 1930 match against Ireland, partnered by Gilbert Alexander on the latter's home ground; and again in 1932 he had another century opening stand against the Irish. Moreover, another opening stand, of 59 with J.F. Jones, sealed the match against the South Americans. So in this final stage Kerr was useful rather than brilliant; and his last international match was little more successful than his first. He did not bowl in this period, but still picked up some useful catches at slip. His first-class batting average slipped below 40, while that for all international matches was just a shade below that figure; and, as noted above, Kerr's average against Australian sides was above 40. His average in all cricket was at about that level, which perhaps showed that he could raise his game for the occasion, thus displaying temperament as well as technique.

The Statistics (First-Class)

Centuries (4)

178*	v Ireland	at Dublin (Trinity)	1923
137	v Ireland	at Greenock	1926
137	v Ireland	at Edinburgh (RP)	1928
136	v Ireland	at Dublin (Trinity)	1927

Century Stands (6)

203	(1st)	with I.T.Parker	v Ireland	at Greenock	1926
150	(1st)	with G.W.A.Alexander	v Ireland	at Aberdeen	1930
123	(1st)	with A.J.Stevenson	v Ireland	at Dublin (Trinity)	1927
115	(1st)	with A.W.Angus	v Ireland	at Glasgow (HC)	1922
108	(1st)	with J.F.Jones	v Ireland	at Greenock	1932
102*	(2nd)	with J.Grieve	v Ireland	at Edinburgh (RP)	1920

Batting and Fielding against Various Opponents

(For bowling see match analyses)

	M	*I*	*NO*	*R*	*Ave*	*HS*	*100*	*50*	*Ct*
Ireland	16	29	5	1393	58.04	178*	4	8	18
Major tourists (excluding South Americans)	5	9	0	176	19.55	42	0	0	2
Surrey	3	5	0	121	24.20	54	0	1	5
Lancashire	1	2	0	31	15.50	31	0	0	1
Middlesex	1	2	0	12	6.00	7	0	0	0
Nottinghamshire	1	2	0	0	0.00	0	0	0	1
Wales	2	4	0	104	26.00	60	0	1	1
MCC	1	2	0	24	12.00	15	0	0	1
Oxford University	1	2	0	65	32.50	44	0	0	2
South Americans	1	2	1	49	24.50	39*	0	0	0
Total	**32**	**59**	**6**	**1975**	**37.26**	**178***	**4**	**10**	**31**

Batting and Fielding on Various Grounds

(For bowling see match analyses)

	M	*I*	*NO*	*R*	*Ave*	*HS*	*100*	*50*	*Ct*
Edinburgh (RP)	7	13	3	421	42.10	137	1	3	4
Glasgow (HC)	4	8	0	201	25.12	75	0	1	4
Dundee	2	3	0	30	10.00	22	0	0	2
Greenock	2	3	0	219	73.00	137	1	1	4
Perth	2	4	0	130	32.50	60	0	1	2
Aberdeen	1	1	0	88	88.00	88	0	1	1
Dublin (Trinity)	5	10	2	512	64.00	178*	2	1	5
Dublin (Rathmines)	2	4	1	135	45.00	74	0	1	1
Belfast	1	2	0	14	7.00	13	0	0	1
Oval	2	3	0	72	24.00	54	0	1	3
Old Trafford	1	2	0	31	15.50	31	0	0	1
Lord's	1	2	0	24	12.00	15	0	0	1
Oxford	1	2	0	65	32.50	44	0	0	2
Swansea	1	2	0	33	16.50	24	0	0	0
Total	**32**	**59**	**6**	**1975**	**37.26**	**178***	**4**	**10**	**31**

Types of Dismissal

Bowled	11
Caught	27
Lbw	12
Stumped	2
Run out	1
Total	**53**

Main Bowlers Dismissed by

Bowler	*Team*	*Type*	*Dismissals*
T.H.Dixon	Ireland	RFM	4
R.J.H.Lambert	Ireland	OB	3
F.P.Ryan	Wales	SLA	3

James Aitchison

1946-1950

First-Class

	Own	Team Totals	Opp	Bowling	Ct
1 Scotland v Ireland at Glenpark, Greenock, July 13, 15, 16, 1946 Ireland won by eight wickets					
b J.C.Boucher	57	259	326		
c J.Bowden b J.C.Boucher	39	173	108/2		
2 Scotland v Ireland at The Mardyke, Cork, May 31, June 2, 3, 1947 Draw					
b J.C.Boucher	56	140	103		
lbw b N.B.Hool	59	181/9d	106/8		
3 Scotland v Warwickshire at Edgbaston, Birmingham, July 30, 31, 1947 Warwickshire won by four wickets					
c H.E.Dollery b V.H.D.Cannings	9	158	210		
st H.E.Dollery b W.E.Hollies	28	112	62/6		
4 Scotland v Warwickshire at Edgbaston, Birmingham, July 14, 15, 16, 1948 Draw					
c sub b R.H.Maudsley	18	187	306/4d		
c F.C.Gardner b D.Flint	23	160/3	116/2d		
5 Scotland v Ireland at Hamilton Crescent, Glasgow, July 24, 26, 27, 1948 Ireland won by 118 runs					
b N.B.Hool	6	127	137		
b J.C.Boucher	25	133	241		
6 Scotland v Yorkshire at The Circle, Hull, July 1, 2, 3, 1949 Draw					
c W.Watson b E.P.Robinson	36	170	289/1d		
c N.W.D.Yardley b A.Mason	9	89/5			
7 Scotland v New Zealanders at Hamilton Crescent, Glasgow, July 16, 18, 19, 1949 New Zealanders won by ten wickets					
c H.B.Cave b G.O.Rabone	2	137	423		
b J.Cowie	11	299	16/0		
8 Scotland v Ireland at Ormeau, Belfast, July 23, 25, 26, 1949 Ireland won by 73 runs					
c J.Bowden b J.C.Boucher	6	80	134		
c T.N.Newburn b J.C.Boucher	26	134	153		
9 Scotland v Ireland at The North Inch, Perth, June 24, 26, 27, 1950 Draw					
b J.C.Boucher	10	58	118		
c F.J.Miller b R.I.Gill	42	315	213/8		
10 Scotland v Sussex at The County Ground, Hove, July 1, 3, 4, 1950 Draw					
c J.M.Parks b C.Oakes	91	220	302/8d		
lbw b C.Oakes	21	235	90/7		
11 Scotland v Yorkshire at Raeburn Place, Edinburgh, July 12, 13, 14, 1950 Yorkshire won by 196 runs					
lbw b R.Appleyard	2	188	314/9d		
c sub b J.H.Wardle	4	72	142/4d		

	M	I	NO	R	Ave	HS	100	50	O	M	R	W	Ave	BB	Ct
1946-1950	11	22	0	580	26.36	91	0	4	-	-	-	-	-	-	0

Non First-Class

	Own	Team Totals	Opp	Bowling	Ct
A Scotland v Indians at Myreside, Edinburgh, May 22, 23, 1946 Indians won by an innings and 56 runs					
c R.B.Nimbalkar b V.S.Hazare	59	101	247		
b V.S.Hazare	23	90			
B Scotland v Yorkshire at Hamilton Crescent, Glasgow, July 17, 18, 1946 Draw					
b A.Coxon	7	189	60/0		
C Scotland v Yorkshire at Philiphaugh, Selkirk, June 25, 26, 1947 Draw					
b A.Coxon	4	46	213/9d		
not out	71	121/2	93/5d		

D Scotland v South Africans at Whitehaugh, Paisley, July 23, 24, 1947 Draw

not out	106	177	278/4d		
b J.B.Plimsoll	1	104/5			

E Scotland v Australians at Raeburn Place, Edinburgh, September 13, 14, 1948 Australians won by an innings and 40 runs

not out	25	85	236		
b A.R.Morris	5	111			

F Scotland v Australians at Mannofield, Aberdeen, September 17, 18, 1948 Australians won by an innings and 87 runs

c R.R.Lindwall b C.L.McCool	32	178	407/6d		c R.N.Harvey c A.R.Morris
c W.A.Brown b D.Tallon	9	142			

G Scotland v Durham at Ashbrooke, Sunderland, May 30, 31, 1949 Scotland won by eight wickets

c S.Guthrie b R.O.Lowerson	10	247	222		
b D.W.Hardie	0	90/2	114		

H Scotland v Warwickshire at Mannofield, Aberdeen, July 13, 14, 1949 Draw

c R.E.Hitchcock b C.W.L.Grove	32	292/3d	291/6d		c J.S.Ord
c R.T.Spooner b C.W.L.Grove	31	158/6	234/7d		

When Jimmy Aitchison's international career finally began in 1946, he immediately sprang to prominence with a half-century in his first innings against the touring Indians. Then he opened the batting, as he did from time to time in later matches, though he was more often to be found lower down the order. In his maiden first-class match, against Ireland, *Wisden* notes that he was the only Scot to hold out against the spin of Jimmy Boucher; though the latter was to have his revenge in later years. Next year's match against the Irish saw Aitchison score two 'fine' half-centuries in a low-scoring game. In his next match, a non first-class one against Yorkshire, he took his best career score to 71 not out; which he bettered a month later with 106 undefeated against the South Africans, but again in a two-day match. 1948's match against Ireland saw Jimmy fall relatively cheaply to Boucher and Hool, against both of whom he was to fall a number of times. The same year saw him feature in Scotland's two innings defeats against the Australians. In each case he batted down the innings at six, too low considering his reasonable first innings scores. He also took his first two international catches, the notable scalps of Neil Harvey and Arthur Morris. In 1949 a match against Durham, then not a first-class county, saw him being awarded a Scottish cap, though oddly the match in that year against The Army, in which he had an unbeaten 64, was not regarded as a 'cap' international, hence it is not included in the statistics in this book. In the match against Sussex in 1950 Aitchison had his best first-class score so far, but he, and Scotland, failed miserably against Yorkshire.

1951-1954

First-Class

	Own	*Team Totals*	*Opp*	*Bowling*	*Ct*

12 Scotland v Warwickshire at Edgbaston, Birmingham, May 19, 21, 22, 1951 Draw

c E.B.Lewis b R.G.Carter	48	359	332		
did not bat	-	8/0			

13 Scotland v Northamptonshire at Raeburn Place, Edinburgh, June 16, 18, 19, 1951 Draw

c K.Fiddling b V.Broderick	29	323	380		
did not bat	-	169/5			

14 Scotland v Ireland at Trinity College Park, Dublin, June 23, 25, 26, 1951 Scotland won by three wickets

c J.S.Pollock b S.S.J.Huey	108	229	303		
c S.A.Curley b S.S.J.Huey	31	221/7	144/7d		

15 Scotland v Worcestershire at Forthill, Dundee, June 30, July 2, 3, 1951 Worcestershire won by an innings and 50 runs

hit wkt b M.E.Bradley	64	114	351/9d		
st H.Yarnold b M.E.Bradley	44	187			

16 Scotland v Yorkshire at North Marine Parade, Scarborough, July 25, 26, 27, 1951 Yorkshire won by seven wickets

c R.Booth b R.Appleyard	37	121	372/1d		

st R.Booth b E.Leadbeater 74 272 23/3

17 Scotland v Yorkshire at Hamilton Crescent, Glasgow, June 25, 26, 27, 1952 Draw
c D.B.Close b R.Wood 150 381/9d 292 c E.I.Lester
c J.H.Wardle b R.Wood 0 107 116/6

18 Scotland v Ireland at Whitehaugh, Paisley, July 5, 7, 8, 1952 Scotland won by an innings and 18 runs
c F.J.Miller b J.C.Boucher 18 282 138 c E.D.R.Shearer
c E.Ingram
126 c E. Ingram

19 Scotland v Worcestershire at New Road, Worcester, August 6, 7, 8, 1952 Draw
c R.T.D.Perks b R.O.Jenkins 5 40/3 141/6d

20 Scotland v Northamptonshire at Town Ground, Peterborough, July 10, 11, 12, 1953 Draw
st K.V.Andrew b G.E.Tribe 26 66 361/1d
c K.V.Andrew b G.E.Tribe 44 126/4

21 Scotland v Yorkshire at Hamilton Crescent, Glasgow, June 17, 18, 19, 1953 Draw
not out 30 79/1 308

22 Scotland v Derbyshire at Park Road, Buxton, June 2, 3, 4, 1954 Derbyshire won by five wickets
b R.Carter 43 250 240
c H.J.Rhodes b A.Eato 5 100 114/5

23 Scotland v Pakistanis at Raeburn Place, Edinburgh, June 16, 17, 18, 1954 Pakistanis won by ten wickets
b M.E.Z.Ghazali 61 353/7d 295 c Shujauddin
c Mahmood Hussain
b Mahmood Hussain 2 51 114/0

24 Scotland v Ireland at Whitehaugh, Paisley, July 17, 19, 20, 1954 Draw
c A.E.Marks b N.B.Hool 103 489 330 c S.F.Bergin
c J.S.Pollock
156/7 1-1-0-0

25 Scotland v Warwickshire at Courtaulds Ground, Coventry, July 28, 29, 30, 1954 Warwickshire won by 63 runs
st E.B.Lewis b R.T.Weeks 45 161 261/6d c N.F.Horner
c Khaled Ibadulla b R.G.Thompson
0 148 111/1d

	M	*I*	*NO*	*R*	*Ave*	*HS*	*100*	*50*	*O*	*M*	*R*	*W*	*Ave*	*BB*	*Ct*
1951-1954	14	22	1	967	46.04	150	3	3	1	1	0	0	-	-	9
1946-1954	25	44	1	1547	35.97	150	3	7	1	1	0	0	-	-	9

Non First-Class

Own *Team Totals* *Opp* *Bowling* *Ct*

I Scotland v South Africans at Hamilton Crescent, Glasgow, July 11, 12, 1951 Draw
c R.A.McLean b C.B.van Rynefeld
55 115 110/3 c E.A.B.Rowan

J Scotland v Australians at Whitehaugh, Paisley, September 15, 16, 1953 Draw
c D.Tallon b G.B.Hole 13 100/3 377/9d

K Scotland v Australians at Raeburn Place, Edinburgh, September 18, 19, 1953 Draw
b R.G.Archer 9 101 308
lbw b A.K.Davidson 3 88/2

The 1951 match against Ireland marked some milestones for Aitchison. He scored his maiden first-class century, taking part in a sixth-wicket century stand with W.A. Edward; and he fell twice to Huey, as a change from Boucher, though the latter was playing in the match. In the following match, against Worcestershire, Jimmy had two good scores, though they were overshadowed by Outschoorn's double century, Jenkins' bowling and Yarnold's wicket-keeping for the opposition. He also performed well against the visiting South Africans, but in the following Yorkshire match he again found his own good innings surpassed by that of an opponent, Vic Wilson's not out 223. However, in the following year's match against Yorkshire, his 150, coupled with a big third-wicket stand with Taylor, proved invaluable for Scotland. Jimmy also took his maiden first-class catch, in his 17th match; but catches were to come more regularly thereafter. He did little in the two two-day matches against the Australians in 1953, both interfered with by the weather. Against the next tourists, the 1954 Pakistanis, Aitchison had a good half-century in the first innings, but his second-innings failure reflected that of all the Scots batsmen. However, he redeemed himself with a century in the Irish match, and even bowled his maiden first-class over (another maiden), when the match was dead; but his batting efforts over the past four seasons had raised his average into the thirties.

1955-1958

First-Class

	Own	*Team Totals*	*Opp*	*Bowling*	*Ct*
26 Scotland v Lancashire at Old Trafford, Manchester, May 7, 9, 10, 1955 Draw					
b M.J.Hilton	25	164	113/0		
27 Scotland v Worcestershire at Hamilton Crescent, Glasgow, May 21, 23, 24, 1955 Worcestershire won by 197 runs					
c G.Dews b M.J.Horton	81	256	382/4d		
c H.Yarnold b R.T.D.Perks	11	103	174/3d		
28 Scotland v Ireland at Trinity College Park, Dublin, July 23, 25, 26, 1955 Scotland won by an innings and 24 runs					
c L.Warke b C.J.M.Kenny	34	272	153		
			95		
29 Scotland v Derbyshire at Raeburn Place, Edinburgh, August 3, 4, 5, 1955 Derbyshire won by eight wickets					
c A.C.Revill b D.B.Carr	74	289	290		
c D.B.Carr b E.Smith	18	104	105/2		
30 Scotland v Yorkshire at The Circle, Hull, May 16, 17, 1956 Yorkshire won by an innings and 145 runs					
b R.Appleyard	29	145	330/6d		
b J.H.Wardle	6	40			
31 Scotland v Lancashire at Whitehaugh, Paisley, July 11, 12, 13, 1956 Lancashire won by 71 runs					
c and b R.Collins	102	208	185		c M.J.Hilton
c K.J.Grieves b M.J.Hilton	25	170	264/2d		
32 Scotland v Warwickshire at Edgbaston, Birmingham, July 25, 26, 27, 1956 Draw					
c M.J.K.Smith b M.Youll	68	315	188		
b S.S.Griffiths	31	158	245/6	1-0-2-0	
33 Scotland v Lancashire at Old Trafford, Manchester, May 15, 16, 17, 1957 Draw					
c and b M.J.Hilton	22	114	254		
			32/0		
34 Scotland v Yorkshire at Whitehaugh, Paisley, May 29, 30, 31, 1957 Draw					
lbw b D.Wilson	53	261	374		
c M.J.Cowan b R.Appleyard	23	137/3			
35 Scotland v MCC at Mannofield, Aberdeen, July 3, 4, 5, 1957 Draw					
c B.L.Muncer b F.R.Brown	52	384	235/9d		c R.F.T.Patterson c R.L.Whitby
c B.Taylor b C.J.Knott	0	125/9d	257/5		
36 Scotland v Warwickshire at Edgbaston, Birmingham, July 24, 25, 26, 1957 Warwickshire won by an innings and 75 runs					
b J.D.Bannister	6	63	287/5d		
run out	23	149			
37 Scotland v Ireland at Trinity College Park, Dublin, July 27, 29, 1957 Ireland won by 38 runs					
c S.F.Bergin b F.Fee	3	82	139		
b F.Fee	30	92	73		c I.B.J.Wilson
38 Scotland v Yorkshire at Acklam Park, Middlesbrough, June 4, 5, 1958 Yorkshire won by an innings and 129 runs					
c D.E.V.Padgett b R.Appleyard	16	80	288		
c sub b M.J.Cowan	0	79			
39 Scotland v New Zealanders at Hamilton Crescent, Glasgow, July 11, 12, 14, 1958 New Zealanders won by an innings and 32 runs					
c J.W.D'Arcy b A.R.MacGibbon	1	135	286		
b J.T.Sparling	5	119			
40 Scotland v Ireland at Cambusdoon (1), Ayr, July 26, 28, 29, 1958 Draw					
c L.Warke b F.Fee	1	117	136/7d		

	M	I	NO	R	Ave	HS	100	50	O	M	R	W	Ave	BB	Ct
1955-1958	15	26	0	739	28.42	102	1	5	1	0	2	0	-	-	4
1946-1958	40	70	1	2286	33.13	150	4	12	2	1	2	0	-	-	13

Non First-Class

	Own	Team Totals	Opp	Bowling	Ct
L Scotland v MCC at Lord's, London, May 30, 31, 1956 Draw					
c H.P.Sharp b J.Flavell	25	208	334		
lbw b F.R.Brown	28	235/6			
M Scotland v Australians at Hamilton Crescent, Glasgow, September 12, 13, 1956 Draw					
b R.R.Lindwall	100	196	328		
N Scotland v Australians at Mannofield, Aberdeen, September 14, 15, 1956 Australians won by an innings and 126 runs					
c G.R.Langley b J.Wilson	8	111	318		
c and b R.Benaud	2	81			
O Scotland v MCC at Lord's, London, June 9, 10, 1958 Draw					
not out	28	124/4	207		c B.D.Wells
P Scotland v New Zealanders at Philiphaugh, Selkirk, July 10, 1958 Draw					
c J.C.Alabaster b A.M.Moir	58	195/9d	119/9		

The 1955 Derbyshire match saw Aitchison again figure in a century stand in the first innings, but it was in a losing cause. Another 'chanceless' hundred came against Lancashire in the following year, when he exercised 'sound judgement' against the spin of Hilton and Tattersall. Aitchison's 68 in the Warwickshire match enabled him to share in a second-wicket century partnership with Len Dudman. Then followed his century against the Australians. In the 1957 match against Yorkshire, Aitchison was uncharacteristically bogged down when he spent three hours over his half-century, before falling yet again to Appleyard. Another half-century followed against a weak MCC side. However, his second innings 30 was the highest score on either side in the low-scoring match against Ireland. Appleyard had him again in 1958, and Jimmy, in company with his Scottish colleagues, put up a dismal performance against the New Zealanders, despite a good performance by him and them against the tourists in the previous one-day match. His falling to Fee again in the Irish match seemed to be highlighting a vulnerability to spin bowling, despite his earlier success against Hilton and Tattersall.

1959-1963

First-Class

	Own	Team Totals	Opp	Bowling	Ct
41 Scotland v Ireland at Trinity College Park, Dublin, June 13, 15, 16, 1959 Draw					
not out	190	355/4d	318		c T.McCloy c W.R.Hunter
b E.H.Bodell	0	121/4d	81/1	1-0-1-0	
42 Scotland v MCC at Raeburn Place, Edinburgh, June 24, 25, 26, 1959 MCC won by three wickets					
b E.R.Dexter	2	169	142		
c R.T.Webb b G.Goonesena	25	158	186/7		c R.E Marshall c M.P.Murray
43 Scotland v Indians at Whitehaugh, Paisley, July 8, 9, 10, 1959 Draw					
run out	44	261	293		
lbw b P.R.Umrigar	19	153/8	210		c J.M. Ghorpade
44 Scotland v Warwickshire at Edgbaston, Birmingham, July 15, 16, 17, 1959 Scotland won by 53 runs					
c H.J.Latham b R.G.Carter	19	262	180/1d		
c G.L.Benson b H.J.Latham	2	128/6d	157		
45 Scotland v Ireland at Whitehaugh, Paisley, July 9, 11, 12, 1960 Draw					
c L.Warke b S.S.J.Huey	38	183	239		
b K.W.Hope	28	219	114/6		

	Own	Team Totals	Opp	Bowling	Ct
46 Scotland v Ireland at Glenpark, Greenock, July 14, 16, 17, 1962 Scotland won by five wickets					
c O.D.Calhoun b W.H.N.Ferguson	19	118	119		
c S.S.J.Huey b W.H.N.Ferguson	63	251/5	249		
47 Scotland v Warwickshire at Raeburn Place, Edinburgh, July 15, 17, 18, 1963 Draw					
c E.Legard b T.W.Cartwright	8	207/5	308		c B.A.Richardson
48 Scotland v Pakistan Eaglets at Philiphaugh, Selkirk, June 29, July 1, 2, 1963 Draw					
hit wkt b Pervez Sajjad	7	140/5	258		
49 Scotland v MCC at Titwood, Glasgow, July 10, 11, 12, 1963 Draw					
c I.R.Lomax b D.Wilson	1	193	195		c R.A.E.Tindall
			11/2		
50 Scotland v Ireland at Beechgrove, Londonderry, July 27, 29, 1963 Ireland won by 70 runs					
c J.A.O'Meara b W.H.N.Ferguson	0	69	125		c S.F.Bergin
					c W.H.N.Ferguson
c O.D.Calhoun b S.S.J.Huey	35	131	145		

	M	*I*	*NO*	*R*	*Ave*	*HS*	*100*	*50*	*O*	*M*	*R*	*W*	*Ave*	*BB*	*Ct*
1959-1963	10	17	1	500	31.25	190*	1	1	1	0	1	0	-	-	9
1946-1963	50	87	2	2786	32.78	190*	5	13	3	1	3	0	-	-	22

Non First-Class

	Own	*Team Totals*	*Opp*	*Bowling*	*Ct*
Q Scotland v MCC at Lord's, London, August 22, 23, 1960 MCC won by nine wickets					
c J.L.Willatt b P.I.Bedford	17	235	229		
b J.H.Chesterton	1	113	123/1	1-0-4-0	
R Scotland v MCC at Lord's, London, June 6, 7, 1962 Draw					
b D.R.Smith	28	227	201		c D.R.Smith
c J.B.Mortimore b A.Wassell	9	98/6	219/0d		
S Scotland v Middlesex at Raeburn Place, Edinburgh, June 27, 28, 1962 Draw					
not out	78	210	207		
b P.I.Bedford	6	166/9	198/7d		c R.W.Hooker

Non First-Class

	M	*I*	*NO*	*R*	*Ave*	*HS*	*100*	*50*	*O*	*M*	*R*	*W*	*Ave*	*BB*	*Ct*
1946-1962	19	32	5	883	32.70	106*	2	5	1	0	4	0	-	-	7

All matches for Scotland

	M	*I*	*NO*	*R*	*Ave*	*HS*	*100*	*50*	*O*	*M*	*R*	*W*	*Ave*	*BB*	*Ct*
1946-1963	69	119	7	3669	32.75	190*	7	18	4	1	7	0	-	-	29

At Dublin in 1959 Aitchison had his highest first-class score, followed by a duck, and another over. He featured in a third-wicket partnership with Mike Denness, whose first international match this was; and an unbroken stand of 117 for the fifth wicket with Jimmy Allan, who also had a significant career in England with Kent and Warwickshire. The latter side also provided Scotland with a rare, if somewhat fortunate, victory over an English county, though Aitchison himself contributed but little to the win. He played relatively little cricket in 1960 and 1961, as he entered his forties, but in 1962 his third-wicket stand of 99 with Robert Young against Ireland saw Scotland almost to victory, achieved shortly afterwards. That match also saw Jimmy's one thousandth run against Ireland, thus repeating John Kerr's feat. Also in 1962 Aitchison had a third-wicket stand of 125 with Ronnie Chisholm that saw Scotland to a reasonable score in a two-day match against Middlesex. 1963 was Jimmy's last season in international cricket. He played in four matches, but three were ruined by rain; he scored relatively poorly anyway. The Irish match was over in two days, though his final 35 was just above average for his career.

The Statistics (First-Class)

Centuries (5)

190*	v Ireland	at Dublin (Trinity)	1959
150	v Yorkshire	at Glasgow (HC)	1952
108	v Ireland	at Dublin (Trinity)	1951
103	v Ireland	at Paisley	1954
102	v Lancashire	at Paisley	1956

Century Stands (7)

178	(3rd)	with J.A.S.Taylor	v Yorkshire	at Glasgow (HC)	1952
153	(2nd)	with L.C.Dudman	v Warwickshire	at Edgbaston	1956
144	(3rd)	with M.H.Denness	v Ireland	at Dublin (Trinity)	1959
139	(2nd)	with R.H.E.Chisholm	v Ireland	at Paisley	1954
129	(6th)	with W.A.Edward	v Ireland	at Dublin (Trinity)	1951
117*	(5th)	with J.M.Allan	v Ireland	at Dublin (Trinity)	1959
110	(3rd)	with G.W.L.Courtenay	v Derbyshire	at Edinburgh (RP)	1955

Batting and Fielding against Various Opponents

(For bowling see match analyses)

	M	*I*	*NO*	*R*	*Ave*	*HS*	*100*	*50*	*Ct*
Ireland	15	26	1	1027	41.08	190*	3	4	10
Tourists (incl. Pakistan Eaglets)	5	9	0	152	16.88	61	0	1	3
Warwickshire	8	14	0	328	23.42	68	0	1	2
Yorkshire	8	15	1	469	33.50	150	1	2	1
Lancashire	3	4	0	174	43.50	102	1	0	1
Worcestershire	3	5	0	205	41.00	81	0	2	0
Derbyshire	2	4	0	140	35.00	74	0	1	0
Northamptonshire	2	3	0	99	33.00	44	0	0	0
Sussex	1	2	0	112	56.00	91	0	1	0
MCC	3	5	0	80	16.00	52	0	1	5
Total	**50**	**87**	**2**	**2786**	**32.77**	**190***	**5**	**13**	**22**

Batting and Fielding on Various Grounds

(For bowling see match analyses)

	M	*I*	*NO*	*R*	*Ave*	*HS*	*100*	*50*	*Ct*
Edinburgh (RP)	6	10	0	225	22.50	74	0	2	5
Glasgow (HC)	6	11	1	322	32.20	150	1	1	1
Paisley	6	10	0	453	45.30	103	2	1	7
Greenock	2	4	0	178	44.50	63	0	2	0
Aberdeen	1	2	0	52	26.00	52	0	1	2
Ayr	1	1	0	1	1.00	1	0	0	0
Dundee	1	2	0	108	54.00	64	0	1	0
Glasgow (Titwood)	1	1	0	1	1.00	1	0	0	1
Perth	1	2	0	52	26.00	42	0	0	0
Selkirk	1	1	0	7	7.00	7	0	0	0
Dublin (Trinity)	4	7	1	396	66.00	190*	2	0	3
Belfast	1	2	0	32	16.00	26	0	0	0
Cork	1	2	0	115	57.50	59	0	2	0
Londonderry	1	2	0	35	17.50	35	0	0	2
Edgbaston	6	11	0	275	25.00	68	0	1	0
Hull	2	4	0	80	20.00	36	0	0	0
Middlesbrough	1	2	0	16	8.00	16	0	0	0

Scarborough	1	2	0	111	55.50	74	0	1	0
Old Trafford	2	2	0	47	23.50	25	0	0	0
Buxton	1	2	0	48	24.00	43	0	0	0
Coventry	1	2	0	45	22.50	45	0	0	1
Hove	1	2	0	112	56.00	91	0	1	0
Peterborough	1	2	0	70	35.00	44	0	0	0
Worcester	1	1	0	5	5.00	5	0	0	0
Total	**50**	**87**	**2**	**2786**	**32.77**	**190***	**5**	**13**	**22**

Types of Dismissal

Bowled	20
Caught	52
Lbw	5
Stumped	4
Hit wicket	2
Run out	2
Total	**85**

Main Bowlers Dismissed by

Bowler	*Team*	*Type*	*Dismissals*
J.C.Boucher	Ireland	OB	8
R.Appleyard	Yorkshire	OB	5
S.S.J.Huey	Ireland	SLA	4

Aitchison hooks Martin Horton
MCC v Scotland at Lord's in 1962

The Final Analysis

It is possible to draw a few conclusions from the above statistics. Aitchison had rather more centuries and century stands than Kerr, but the difference does not really reflect the difference in the number of matches played. Both players were very severe on the Irish, but Aitchison also had creditable performances against the two 'Roses' sides, and centuries against the touring Australians and South Africans. Kerr played very creditably in his various encounters with Australian sides; the tourists showed approbation of both players. John also did well on Scottish grounds, though he shared a liking with Aitchison for the Trinity College ground in the heart of Dublin. Kerr appeared but once at Lord's, his two innings producing 24 runs. Aitchison appeared there four times, his 136 runs yielding an average of 22.67.

As noted earlier, John Kerr seems to have fallen leg before rather frequently in his later career, but his reputation as a good runner between the stumps is borne out by only one run out in 59 innings. Aitchison's claim to be a relatively infrequent lbw victim seems to have been ratified by his career statistics. However, he was caught out in about 60% of his dismissals. It is clear that, while he dealt capably with pace bowling, he was vulnerable to spin bowlers, especially if they came from Ireland or Yorkshire. Despite some early success for Aitchison against Jimmy Boucher, the wily Irishman had his revenge. Indeed Boucher had John Kerr as one of his early international victims. Like Kerr, Aitchison seems to have been reasonably safe between the wickets. His two hit-wicket dismissals may have been a statistical freak, rather than due to any failure in technique.

As a regular, and safe, slip fielder, it is not surprising that John had more catches than Jimmy, who sometimes fielded farther out, where he was noted for his accurate returns to the stumps. Kerr was a useful bowler to turn to when a stand was proving obdurate, but he seems to have avoided long spells. Aitchison, despite the claims by his club colleagues, was not really a bowler at international level, only getting an over or two when a match was effectively dead. As noted above, he was never captain of Scotland, whereas Kerr was captain in almost half the matches he played.

Perhaps the most obvious difference between the two, as far as the casual observer was concerned, would have been in their height and build. 'Wee man' Kerr was just that: barely five feet six inches tall, and quite stocky. On the other hand, Jimmy Aitchison was 6ft, weighing 11st 7lb, and fairly slimly built.

It can be seen that there were various differences between Kerr and Aitchison, but there were also similarities. Both came from cricketing families and had been well coached by their club professionals, for whom they had the highest regard. They might well have opted to pursue other sports with as much success, but Kerr and Aitchison chose cricket. Both had started out as predominantly off-side batsmen, but, when bowlers began to cramp their style on that side, they developed their leg-side play. Both could dig in or push the score along, as the situation required.

Oddly, each had as a contemporary in the Scottish side a bowler who was one of the best of his type in Scottish cricketing history. Alongside Kerr was Arbroath CC's Robert Sievwright, a top-class slow left-armer, who had 65 wicket in first-class cricket at 19.96 each. In the earlier part of Aitchison's career, Scotland had a fine pace bowler in George Youngson. From Aberdeenshire CC, Youngson took 75 first-class wickets at 24.81, and, somewhat freakishly, topped the UK first-class bowling averages in 1947, while Denis Compton topped the batting ones.

Kerr and Aitchison were both regarded as hard and single-minded characters in cricket in general and batting in particular. Thus at times they may have seemed rather remote to their colleagues: a charge that has of course been levelled against quite a number of noted batsmen. At any rate, each played vital innings when his country was in danger of defeat. However, neither was consistently brilliant, for each was liable to a run of small scores. Each declined significantly in performance over the age of 40, but it has to be said that then there was probably nobody around to replace them.

Both were stalwarts for their clubs over a long period. However, it has to be noted that, while John Kerr was simply contributing to the success of the Greenock Club which had been very successful before him, and has continued to be so up to the present, Jimmy Aitchison's years at Kilmarnock were the golden ones for the Club; they had not had a great deal of success before him, and since his retirement have suffered vicissitudes both on and off the field of play.

Apart from their cricket lives, both John Kerr and Jimmy Aitchison devoted much time to the Church of Scotland. Kerr seems to have devoted as much time and effort to the Church in its various facets as a layman could be expected to; while Aitchison of course was in the full-time ministry. They left their mark there, but it is perhaps for their cricket that they will both be remembered, for their exploits are still remembered in Scottish cricket long after they left the field of play: stalwarts without whose help Scotland's cricketing performances would have been significantly the poorer. Scottish cricket could still do with their like, as it tries to raise its profile in the world game.

Acknowledgements

Most importantly, for help given towards my task, my sincere thanks must go to the officials and supporters of Greenock CC and Kilmarnock CC, the home clubs of Kerr and Aitchison respectively. I am also most indebted for the help given by Mr Howard Smith of Aberdeenshire CC and Mr Neil Leitch, the statistician of Cricket Scotland. Except where otherwise stated, these clubs and Cricket Scotland have been the provenance of the photographs. Steven Sheen for editing, Catherine Aitchison for supplying information and photographs, David Kelly and Andrew Lamb for proof-reading. I am also grateful for the help of staff and use of facilities at the following:

The Dick Institute, Kilmarnock
Edinburgh Central Library
The General Register Office for Scotland, Edinburgh
The Mitchell Library, Glasgow
St Andrews University Library
The Watt Library, Greenock

Reference was made to the following books:

Rev J. Aitchison: *Kilmarnock Cricket Club: One Hundred Not Out*: Kilmarnock, 1952
P. Bailey, P. Thorn, P. Wynne-Thomas: *Who's Who of Cricketers*: London, 1984
J.S. Carruthers: *The Story of Cricket in Scotland*: Dunlop, 1950
J.G. Farmer (ed.): *The Golden Years: 1952-1976*: Kilmarnock, 1977
R.C. Kelman (ed.): *Aberdeenshire Cricket Club Centenary*: Aberdeen, 1957
R.W.S. Miller: *Scottish Cricketers: 1905-1980*: Cleethorpes, 1981
A. O'Neil: *Annals of Brechin Cricket*: Brechin, 1927
D.W. Potter: *The Encyclopaedia of Scottish Cricket*: Manchester, 1999
T.C. Riddell (ed.): *Greenock Cricket Club: One Hundred Years*: Greenock, 1962
F. Simm: *Saltire and Flannels*: Stow, c 2000
Dr N.L. Stevenson: *Play!*: Edinburgh, 1946

Reference was also made to relevant issues of the following:

The Church of Scotland Year-Book
The Evening Times
The [Glasgow] Herald
The Greenock [Post Office] Directory
The Greenock Telegraph
The Kilmarnock Standard
Life and Work
The Scotsman
The Scottish Cricket Record /Annual/Guide
Wisden Cricketers' Almanack

The websites of CricketArchive and Cricket Scotland were invaluable sources. Where there was a conflict between sources, I exercised my own judgement on each occasion, and accept full responsibility for any errors resulting from that judgement. The Scottish representative side is generally referred to as 'Scotland', and touring sides by their modern titles.

Sincere thanks are also due to The Association of Cricket Statisticians and Historians for their willingness to publish this work.

**Aitchison plays Richard Bowman
in the MCC v Scotland match in 1962 at Lord's**